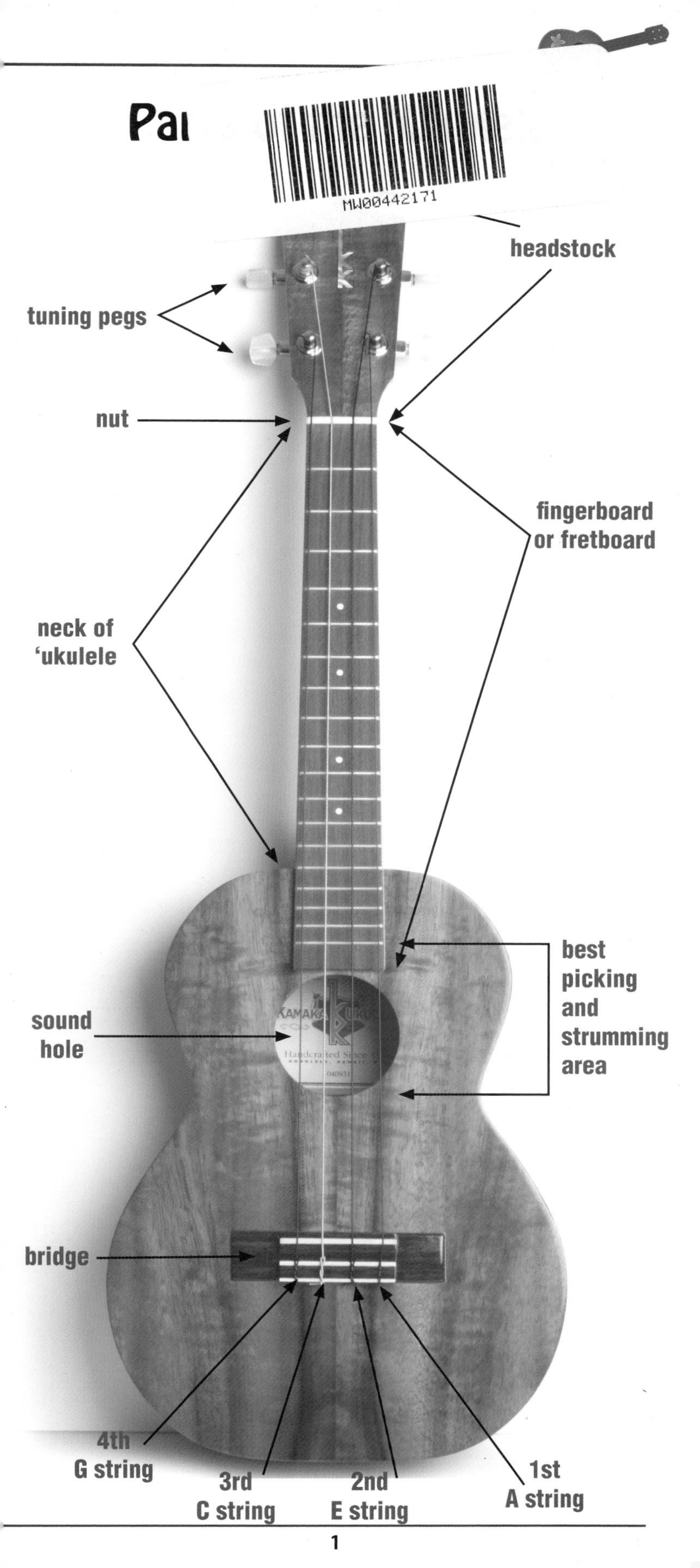
Pa
headstock
tuning pegs
nut
fingerboard
or fretboard
neck of
'ukulele
best
picking
and
strumming
area
sound
hole
bridge
4th
G string
3rd
C string
2nd
E string
1st
A string

Holding and Strumming the 'Ukulele

The picture shows you the best position to hold the 'ukulele. Your right forearm pins it against you, about half way down your chest, on your right. The left hand holds the neck of the 'ukulele and the hand is positioned to bring the fingers over to play notes and chords. Tuck your left elbow in a little, but not tightly.

You can also play sitting down. The curved bottom of the sound box can rest on your thigh which may be easier for some beginners. The thumb of your left hand can either rest under the neck of the 'ukulele or come round a little, as in this lower picture.

Standard or Soprano 'Ukulele

This is the most common size. All four strings are nylon. It is strung G (above middle C), C, E and A. It has a bright high sound.

The whole soprano, from tip of neck to end of soundbox is about **21 inches in length.**

Vibrating String length: ~ is up to 14 inches long.

This is the more accurate way to tell. It is the length of the string from the nut, where the fingerboard begins, to the bridge.

Concert 'Ukulele

The concert is a little longer. The total length is **about 23 inches.**

The ~ string length is between 14 ½ and 16 inches.

The sound box is usually a bit bigger for more volume and sometimes rounded underneath, for better tone. Nylon strings are used but many players put a wound string on the G to drop it an octave. Sometimes the C string is the wound string. This gives the 'ukulele a richer, fuller sound. As the fingerboard is longer, there is a little more space to place the fingers. If you have big hands you should consider this as the minimum size.

Tenor 'Ukulele

The Tenor 'Ukulele is approximately **26 inches.** long. Like the Concert 'Ukulele, it has more frets, enabling one to play a higher melody line.

The ~ string length is usually 17 to 18 inches.

The Tenor is the preferred model of many professional musicians for two reasons:

1. The neck is noticeably longer giving more room for the left hand.

2. The sound production is louder with richer deep notes and a mellow tone overall.

Tuning your 'Ukulele G, C, E, A

Most 'ukulele players today use a small electronic tuner.

This clips on the end of the 'ukulele. Cost: from $7.00-$20.00

'Ukulele Tuning

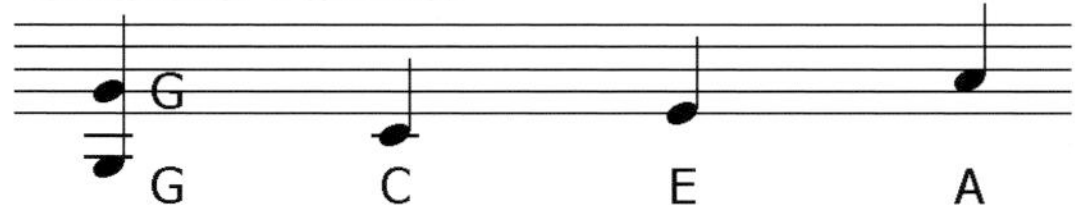

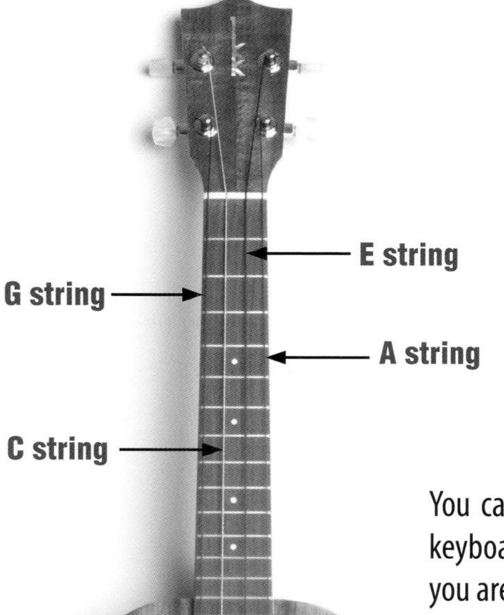

You can also tune from a piano, keyboard, or even by ear! When you are playing in a group always tune everyone to the reference (piano etc,) not to each other, or like Chinese whispers, the tuning can slowly change as you go along the line!

Putting on New Strings

A. Slotted Bridges: Knot the string and pull it tight into the correct slot.

B. Peg Bridges: A few 'ukuleles have pegs. Knot the string and "peg" it into the correct hole.

C. Bridges with holes:

1. Pass the correct string through correct hole in the bridge.
2. Bring it back to loop around the string.
3. Wind it around itself at least twice.
4. Trim to leave about ¼" extending. Wind on peg and pull tight.

 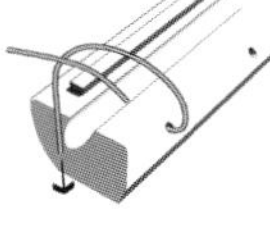 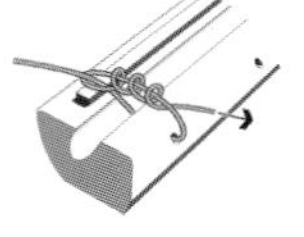 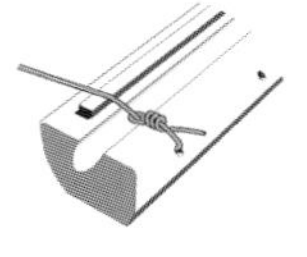

A new string will always stretch. You can speed up stability by gently pre-stretching: Gently tugging the string when it's tightened up and retuning. Repeat about three times.

The Wound, Low G String is substituted by many 'ukulele players so that they can play the melody deeper, below middle C, and also get a richer chord sound.

'Ukulele Tuning

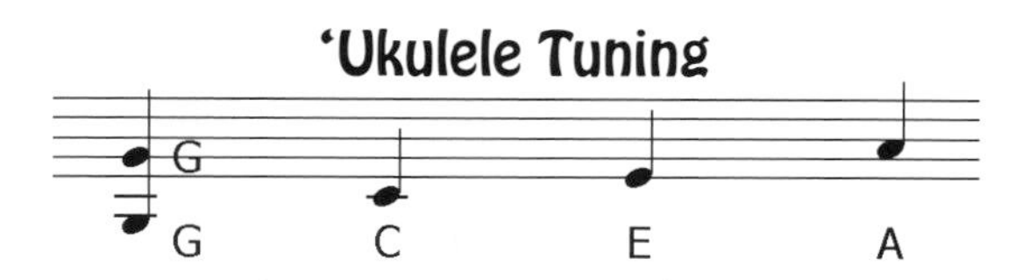

This is why you see **two G notes** notated above. The higher, nylon G is usual on the Soprano and Concert models.

In 'ukulele stores in Hawai'i, you can buy wound G strings specially made for Tenor 'ukulele, (which are fine for the Concert too).

A Classical Guitar, D or 4th string, can also be used. **Make sure it is wound on nylon** (not a steel core), or you'll get a horrible twanging and possibly damage your 'ukulele with too much tension!

ʻUkulele Strumming Introduction

The cheerful and charming sound of the ʻukulele comes partly from its size and tuning, and partly from its wonderful rhythmic possibilities.

As with any stringed instrument, your left and right hands bring out two different and essential qualities. Your left hand creates the musical shapes-chords and melody. Your right hand 'releases' or sends out the melody or chord sounds, by strumming or plucking in many ways.

Chords can be 'sent out' in many ways. They can be strummed very softly and evenly, they can be finger-picked, bringing out each individual string sound, or they can be strummed with energetic rhythms of all kinds.

This book will introduce many strumming and finger picking techniques which will be introduced with particular songs as examples, but once learned, you can adapt and use the techniques to suit the music styles you want to play.

Understanding Chord Diagrams

When chords are presented you will see a grid like this:

The horizontal spaces between the lines represent the frets on the 'ukulele.

The vertical lines represent the strings. The dots on the strings (see next page) are the finger positions to hold down the strings.

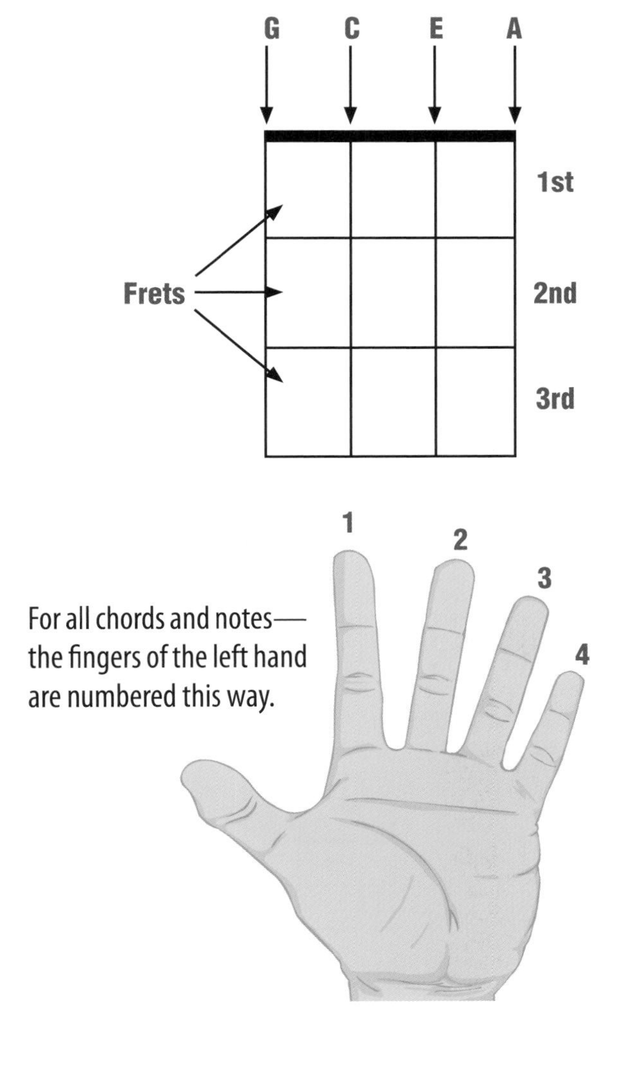

For all chords and notes—the fingers of the left hand are numbered this way.

Left-Hand-Playing the First Chords

Creating harmony is one of the most enjoyable elements of music.

You will be able to accompany yourself and others with chords on the 'ukulele very soon.

To play the simplest chord, the C chord, place your **third finger** down on the **first (A) string,** third fret. Whenever a new chord is taught you will also see a photograph showing the correct position of hand and fingers.

The C chord uses one finger.

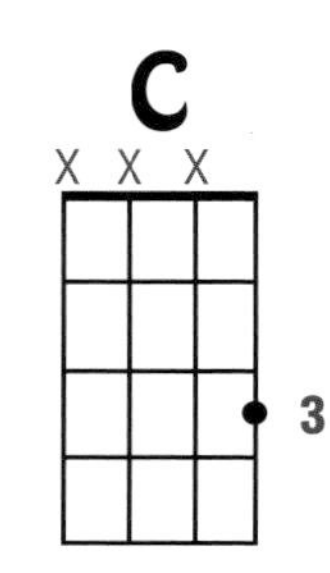

The F chord uses two fingers.

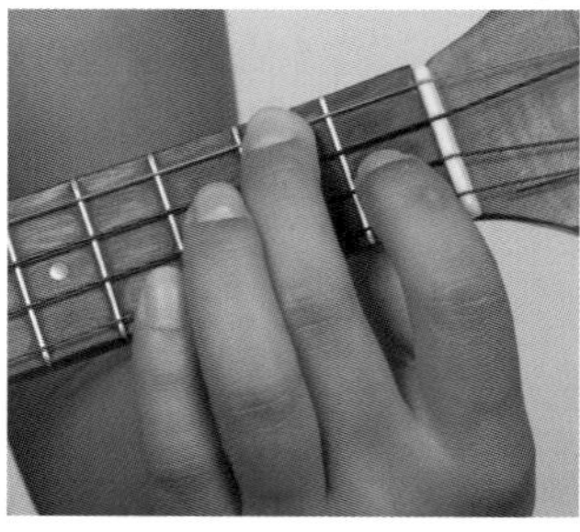

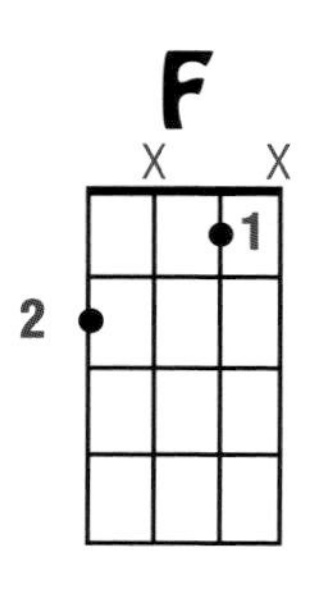

The G7 chord uses three fingers.

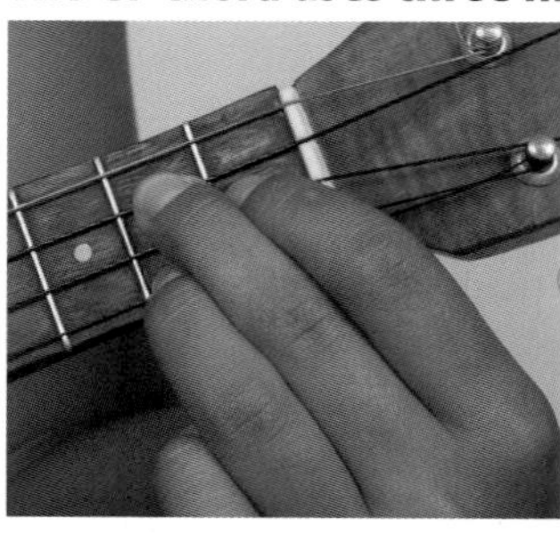

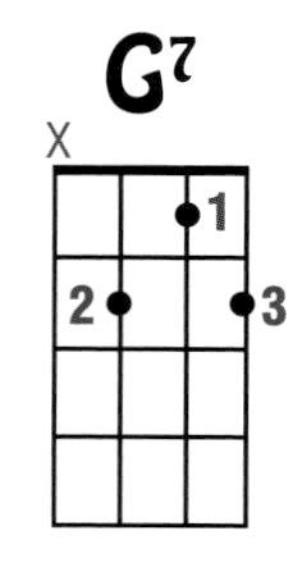

On the next page you will see how to practice these three chords.

Make sure you get a clean sound.

If a note sounds muffled or "fuzzy" it is because you are not pressing it down onto the fingerboard fully.

If this happens build the chord by putting one finger down, making sure it sounds clean, then the next and so on.

When all notes sound clean you can strum them musically.

Practice will soon make this happen easily!

A Rhythm Approach to Learning Chords

Using six different rhythms you will progress from strumming each chord EIGHT times to eventually strumming each chord only ONCE before changing to the next chord!

This approach allows the brain plenty of time to absorb the finger pattern and retain it as "finger memory."

If you can make clean chord changes every two strums (March Time) you are really close to mastery!

1st Exercise—Eight Beats

Strum each chord 8 x before moving to next chord.

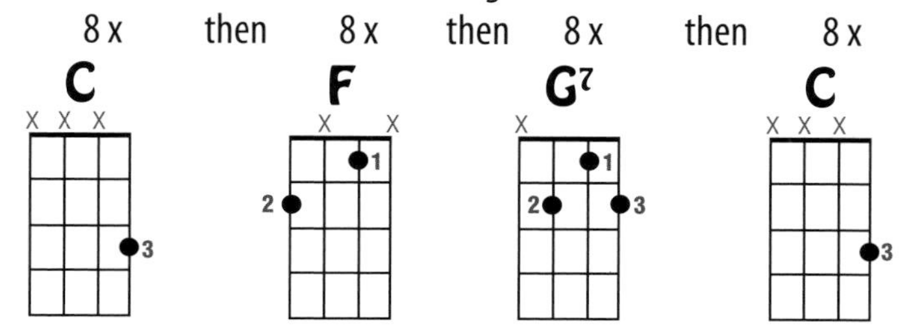

2nd Exercise—Six Beats (double waltz rhythm)

Strum each chord 6 x before moving to the next chord.

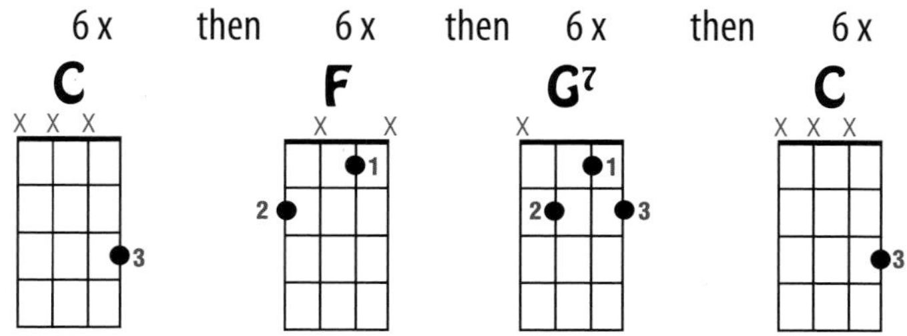

3rd Exercise—Four Beats (pop or jazz rhythm)

Strum each chord 4 x before moving to the next chord.

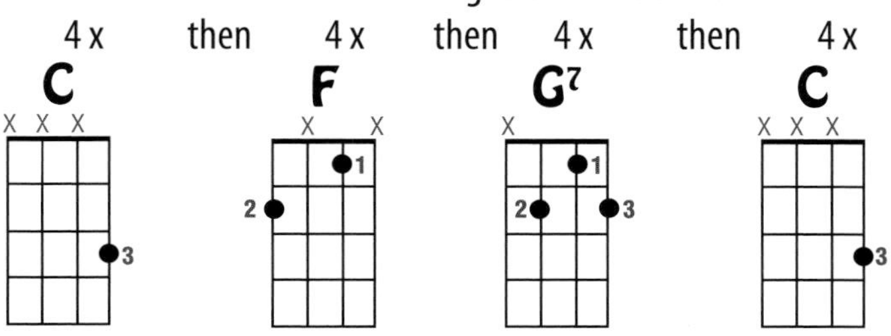

4th Exercise—Three Beats (Waltz rhythm)

Strum each chord 3 x before moving to the next chord.

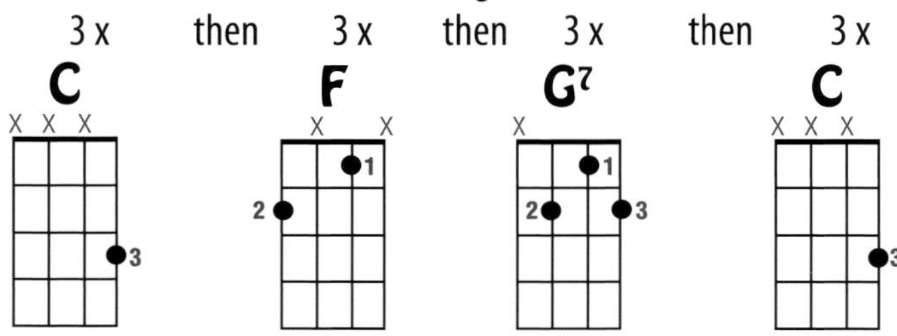

5th Exercise—Two Beats (March rhythm)

Strum each chord 2 x before moving to the next chord.

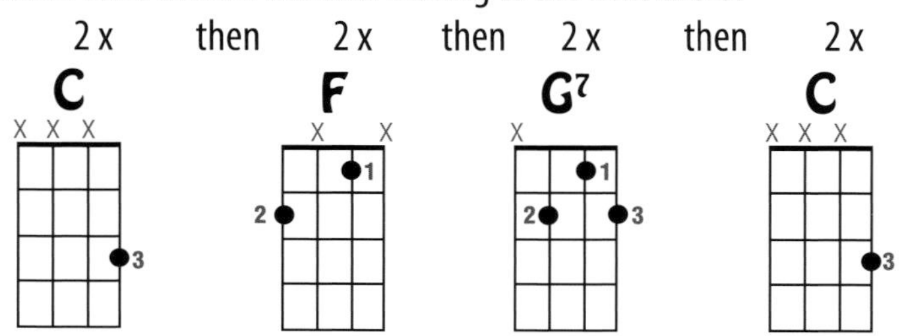

6th - Final Exercise—One Beat (Show-off rhythm!)

Strum each chord 1 x before moving to the next chord

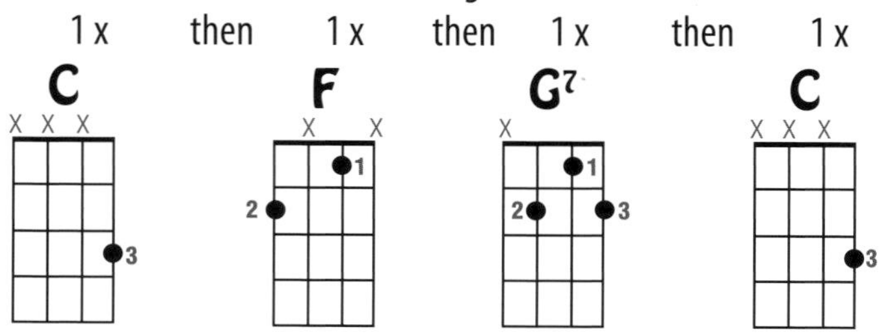

In each lesson a new chord family will be introduced.

Use this same practice sequence with the new chords before you move on to accompanying the songs!

Strumming and Finger Picking—Introduction

Strumming basics: Many beginners strum with stiff fingers and it sometimes takes them a while to learn to relax! Don't use a pick! Your first finger is all that is needed at first!

THE MOST IMPORTANT SECRET!

Keep your right hand very relaxed! Keep your thumb limp and parallel to your hand (see below).

Use your first finger as the strummer, not a pick.

As you go down you should strike the strings with the right (lower) side of your fingernail and finger pad. As you come back up, you should strike with the left (upper) side of the pad of your finger.

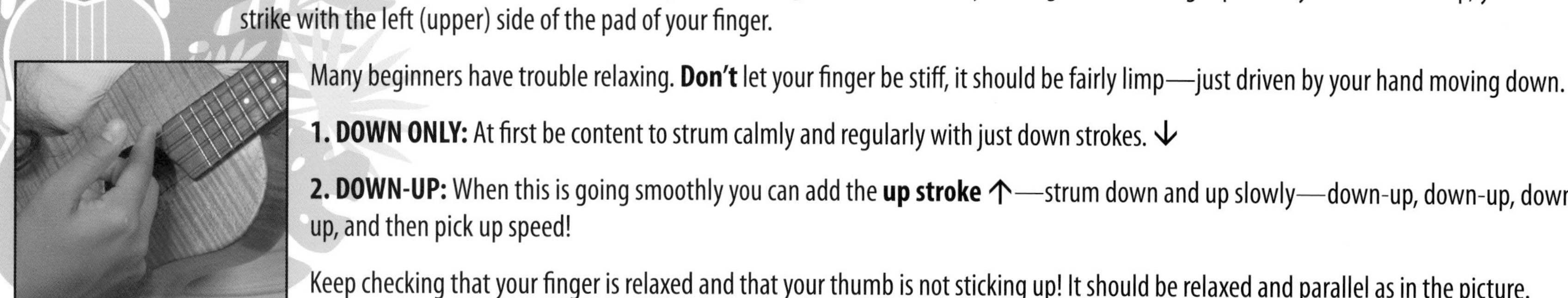

Many beginners have trouble relaxing. **Don't** let your finger be stiff, it should be fairly limp—just driven by your hand moving down.

1. DOWN ONLY: At first be content to strum calmly and regularly with just down strokes. ↓

2. DOWN-UP: When this is going smoothly you can add the **up stroke** ↑—strum down and up slowly—down-up, down-up, down-up, and then pick up speed!

Keep checking that your finger is relaxed and that your thumb is not sticking up! It should be relaxed and parallel as in the picture.

This is a basic introduction to note value when you read music.

About Note Value

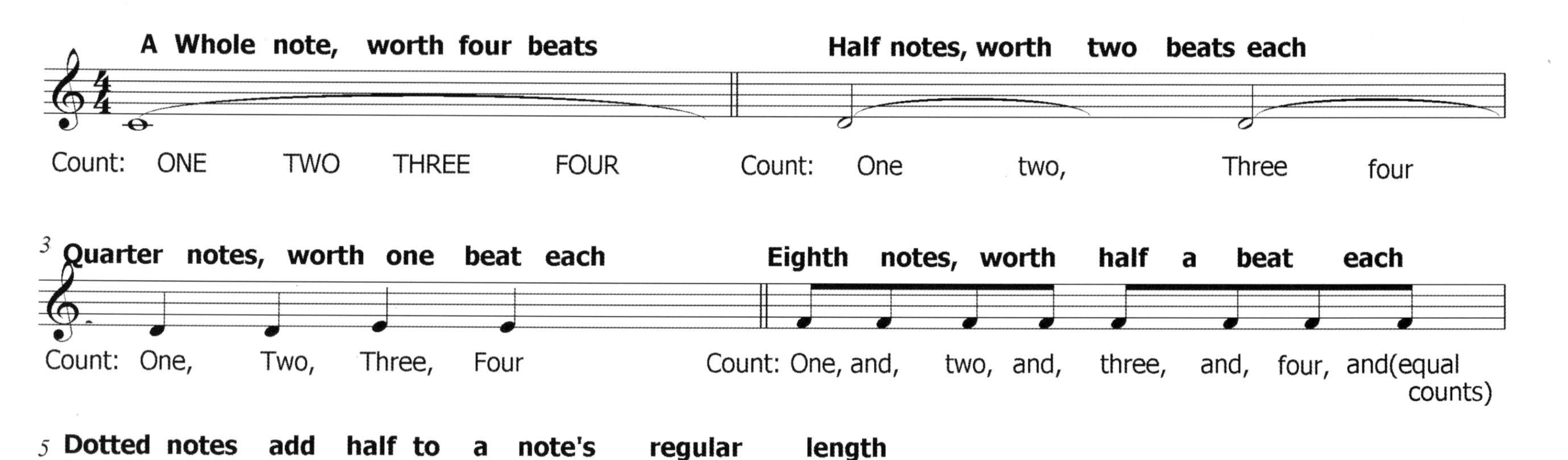

COMMON TIME SIGNATURES: Time signatures will tell how a tune is counted and its rhythm.

The most common times you will see in Hawaiian music are 4/4 , 3/4, and 6/8 . Each of these can be strummed as written, or often "double strummed"—meaning a Down ↓ and Up ↑ strum for each beat.

Each tune in this book will have examples and suggestions for different strum patterns.

Common Time Signatures

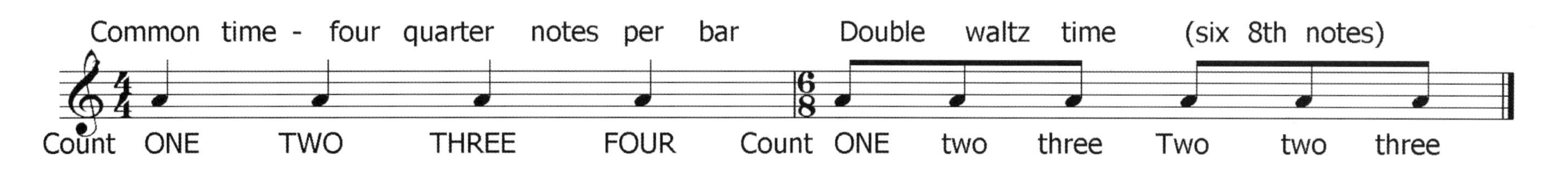

Practice with soft down-strums for this old English melody. It is in 3/4, or slow waltz time—so three strums to each measure.

Drink to Me Only with Thine Eyes

Words - Ben Jonson 1616

English Traditional

Introducing Key and Chords of F

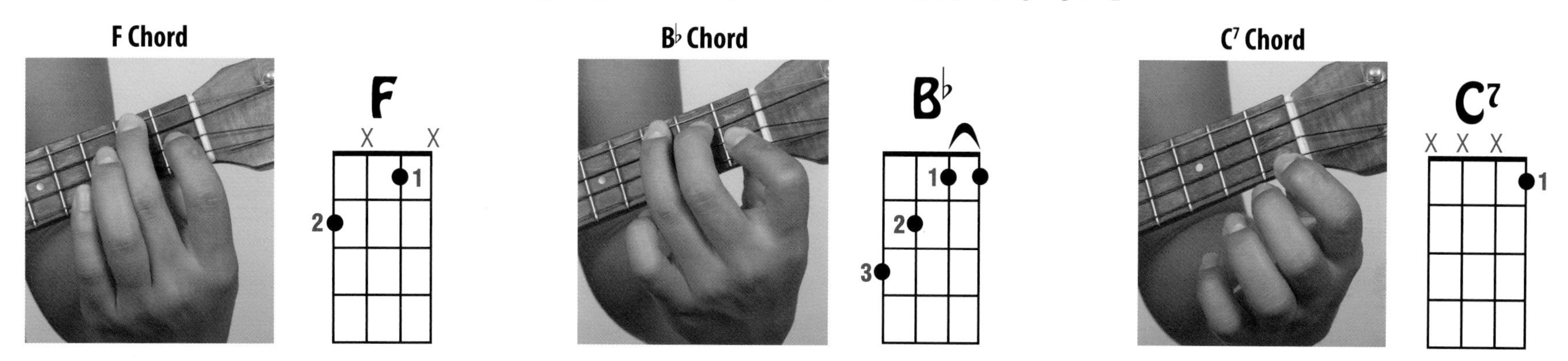

Practice these chords using the same sequence 8 x, 6 x, 4 x, 3 x, 2 x, 1 x (down strums only).

↓ ↑ ... ↓ ↑ ↓ ↑

Then **Down-up** strums 8 x (each one is a down-up strum)—count **one and, two and** etc.

A note on the B♭ chord! Don't be put off by this chord. It is one of the most difficult chords for beginners to master because you have to hold the first two strings down with your first finger. Don't be discouraged if you get a muffled sound at first, it takes time to get a little more finger muscle to do this, so all the strings ring clearly. Almost all of the main chords you will use are easy to hold down. This one is the only challenge! **Try the new chords in this well-known folk song!**

Playing in 3/4 time with some up-strums: This is Hawai'i's state anthem, with words composed by King Kalākaua.

In the measures with three quarter notes just strum down ↓. When there are 8th notes you can add up-strums ↑. See the symbols below on the first four measures. Use the same pattern for the whole song. (Kamehameha [Hawaiian] School choir on YouTube [in white with leis] harmonizes a beautiful rendition of this song!)

Hawai'i Pono'i

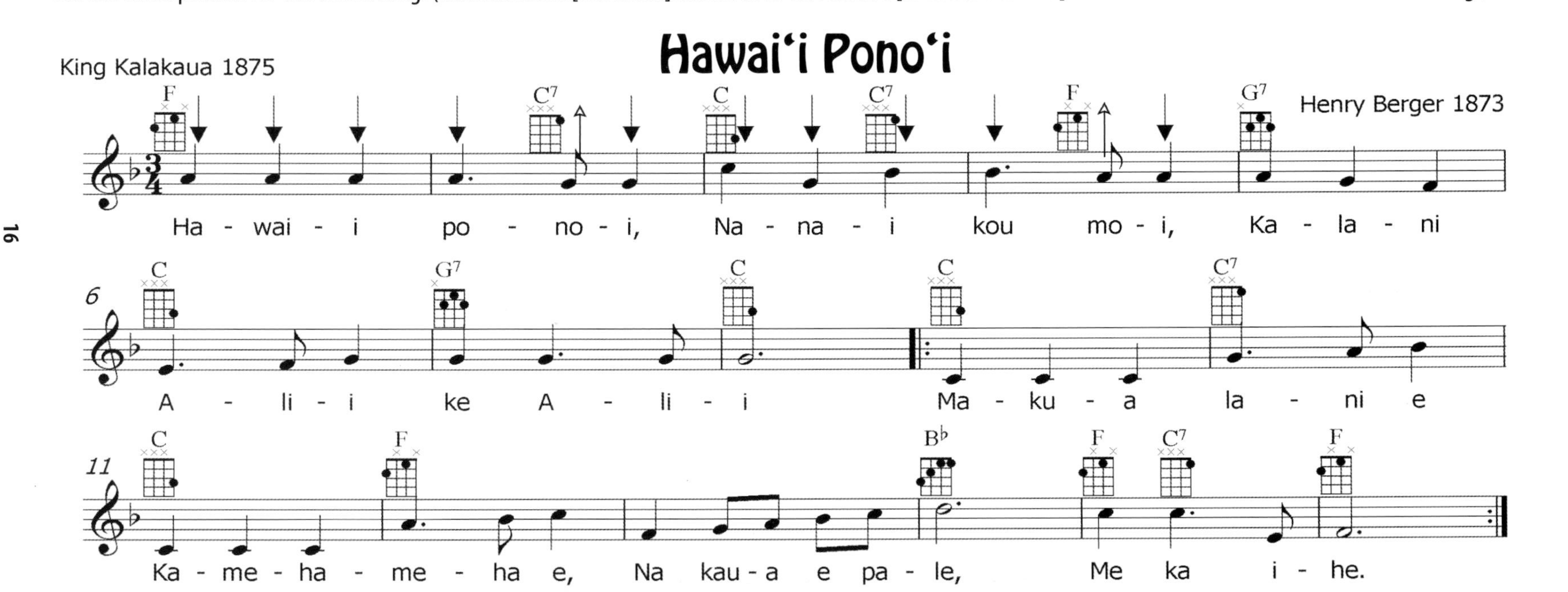

Chords in the Key of D Minor

Every major key has its relative minor key (three notes down), so D minor is the relative key of F major (F → E → D). They share the same key signature. These chords are often found in tunes set in the main key of F.

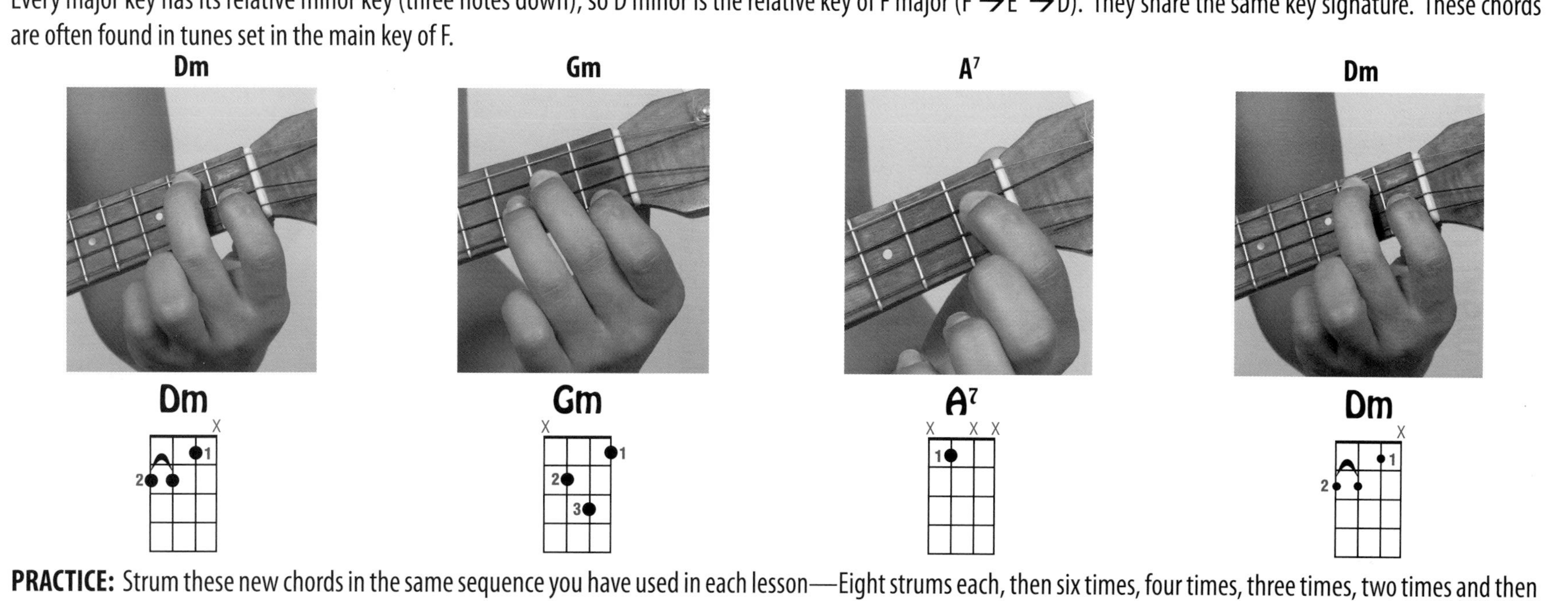

PRACTICE: Strum these new chords in the same sequence you have used in each lesson—Eight strums each, then six times, four times, three times, two times and then one strum each will show mastery of quick change between each chord.

Finger Picking Chords

Often thought of as a strumming instrument, the 'ukulele can be the sweetest and most charming accompanist to singing or other instruments when the chords are **picked** in a rhythmic pattern. This is known as chord finger picking. There are many patterns. Once you get comfortable with some basic ones you can make up your own.

To start, the simplest pattern in 4/4 time is given. In order to do this effectively use your **Thumb** for down ↓ strokes and **1st (index) finger** for **up** ↑ strokes. **Look at the pictures and diagrams to see how the sequence goes.**

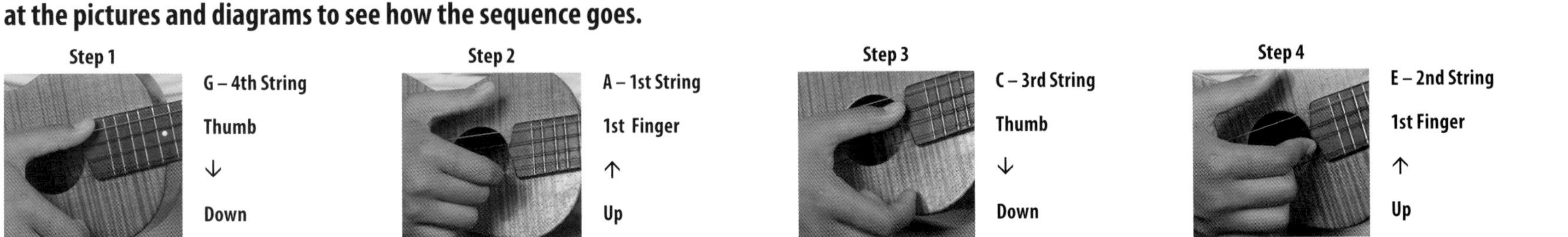

The Thumb plays the 4th and 3rd strings, **the Index** plays the 1st and 2nd strings. The string playing order is: 4↓, 1↑, 3↓, 2↑.

Finger order: Thumb → 1st → Thumb → 1st . Another way to remember is: **The two outer strings (top and bottom) are played first, then the two inner strings.** The Thumb is always on the down beat. Count 1 and 2 and 3 and (the numbers are down, the "ands" are up!).

Practice very slowly and accurately just on one chord until finger memory begins to establish. Then practice the C F G^7 sequence (double on each chord—so: Down-up, down-up, down-up, down-up) and repeat before moving to the next chord. You will soon pick up speed!

Try your hand at finger picking in 4/4 time to this lovely song which Elvis Presley put out as "Love me Tender."
There will be a down-up (you'll pick two strings) on each quarter note, double this on half notes like "spring," "Lee," etc.

Aura Lee

Traditional

Strumming and Finger Picking the Chords of G Major

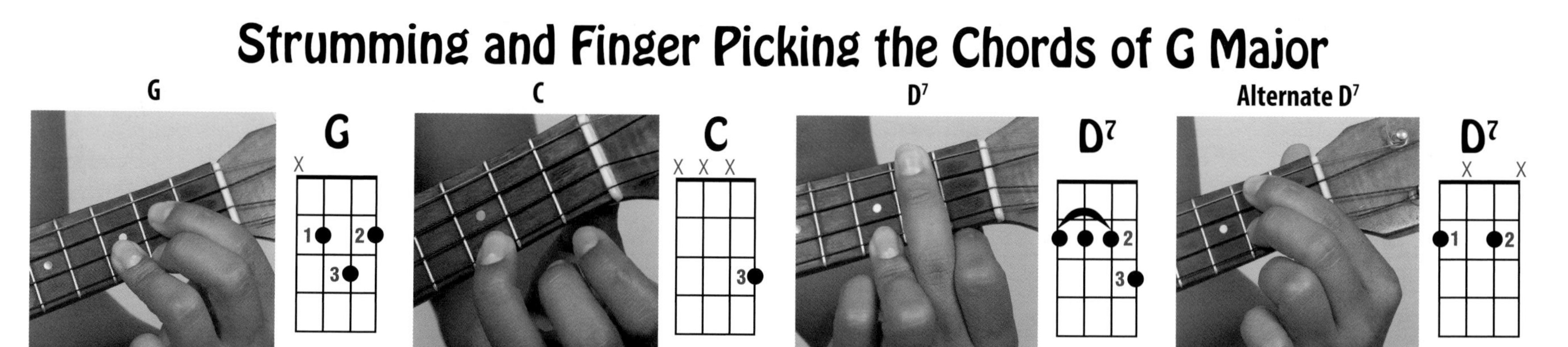

Strumming for finger memory: Strum these chords in the same 8 x, 6 x, 4 x, 3 x, 2 x,1 x sequence as before. Then practice up-down strums (twice as many). The alternate D^7 is easier to play, but sometimes the first or second D^7 suits a harmony better, so learn both!

Finger picking: Once your fingers are familiar with the chord shapes try them with 4/4 finger picking.

Do the finger picking sequence for each chord, twice at first, like this: (string numbers) 4↓ 1↑ 3↓ 2↑, 4↓ 1↑ 3↓ 2↑, **or counting: "One**-and-**Two**-and-**Three**-and-**Four**-and-", " **One**-and-**Two**-and-**Three**-and-**Four**-and-", before changing to the next chord.

The next song is fun for strumming practice with the new chords of G and D^7. You can hear a fine version of this by Woodie Guthrie online.

Mr. Rabbit, Mr. Rabbit
Four Part Round
African American Spiritual
Each part enters here - (Mr...)
G
Mist- er Rab- bit, Mist- er Rab- bit- your ears are might- y long!
4
G D7 G
Yes my Lord they're put on wro__ ng. Ev'- ry lit- tle soul must
7
D7 G G D7 G
shine, shine, shi- ne! Ev' ry lit- tle soul must shi- ne, Strum shine, shine!

The Chords of D Major—with Alternate A^7

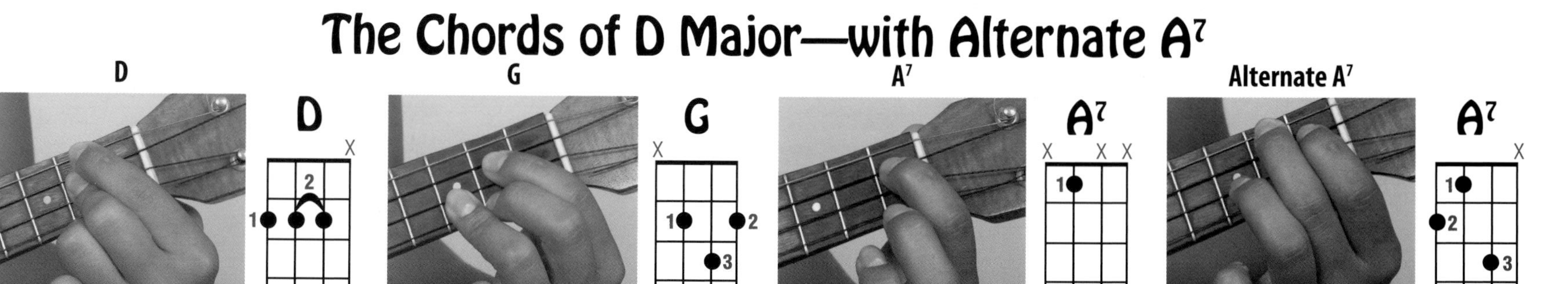

1. Practice these chords with the same 8 x, 6 x, 4 x, 3 x, 2 x, and 1 x rhythm (choose which A^7 chord you will use).

2. Then try them with 4/4 finger picking. Do each chord 2 x at first, like this: ↓4 ↑1 ↓3 ↑2, ↓4 ↑1 ↓3 ↑2, or **counting:**

One-and-Two-and-Three-and-Four-and, One-and-Two-and-Three-and-Four-and, then change to the next chord.

Now, play each chord with only one 4/4 finger picking sequence. When this is going smoothly, go to the next page and try your hand at **"My Grandfather's Clock"** which, like a clock, has a very steady 4 /4 "tick-tock" rhythm!

But first! A note on **Pick-up Beats: Many if not most folk tunes have a pick-up beat which leads into the first full measure.** So in "**My Grandfather's Clock,"** you would count **1, 2, 3, 4 to set the speed** then 1, 2, 3 and on **4** you'd sing or play **"My"** (the 4th beat and the pick-up note), leading to the first full measure with **Grand** being the downbeat.

Finger Picking in the Key of G—4/4 time.

Try finger-picking this well-known folk song in the **Key of G. Two** strings are plucked on the quarter notes (example: above **"grand"** in measure 2) and one on each 8th note. When you play the G chord above **"stopped"** (measure 14) this will last all four strings!

My Grandfather's Clock

Minor Chords for the Key of G

Em

Am

B⁷

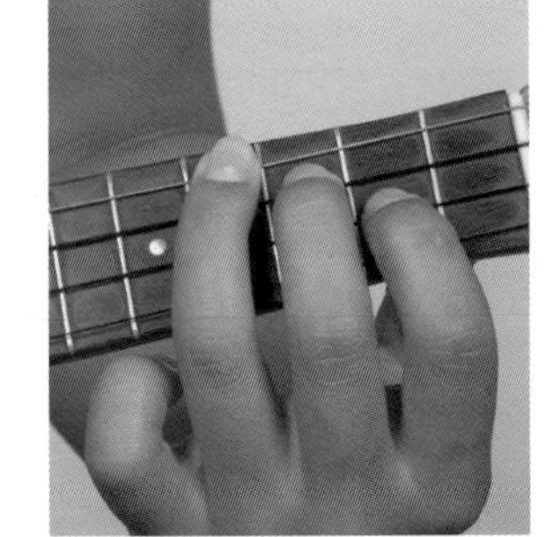

Em

Am

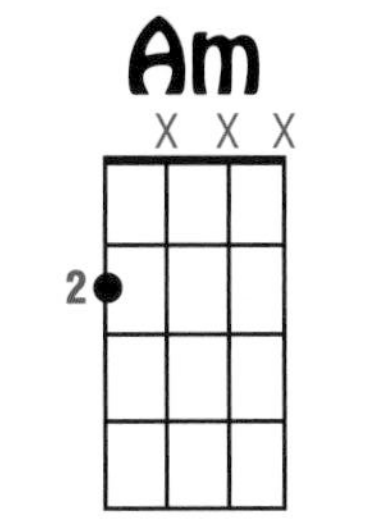

B⁷

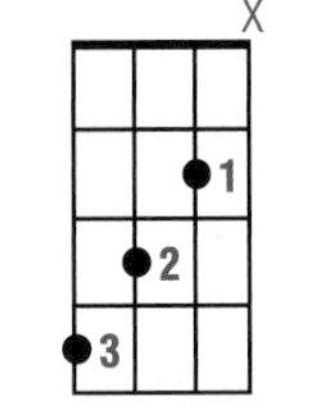

The A minor chord is very easy and only has the 2nd finger down.

The E minor and B^7 chords have exactly the same finger pattern. If playing the E minor chord, you just move one string across to the left to play the B^7 chord.

Use the same 8 x, 6 x, 4 x, 3 x, 2 x,1 x sequence to learn and fix in finger memory these chords.

Finger picking rhythm for 3/4 , 6/4, or 6/8 time uses a different pattern to 4/4 finger picking.

Count like this: One, Two, And Three, And—or with fingers: Down↓ Down↓ Up↑ Down↓ Up↑ (thumb is every down).

→
4th String G
Thumb
Down ↓

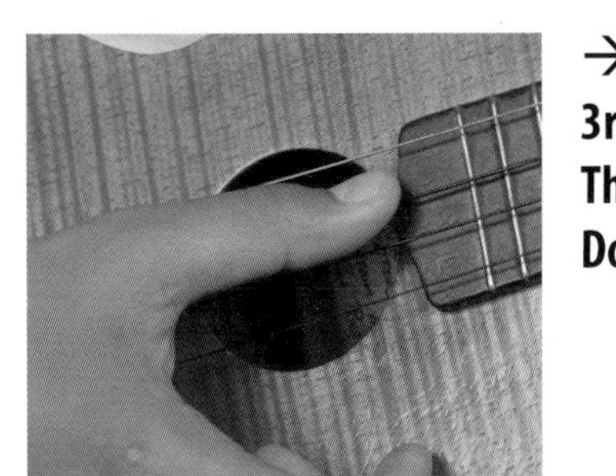

→
3rd String C
Thumb
Down ↓

→
1st String A
1st Finger
Up ↑

→
2nd String E
Thumb
Down ↓

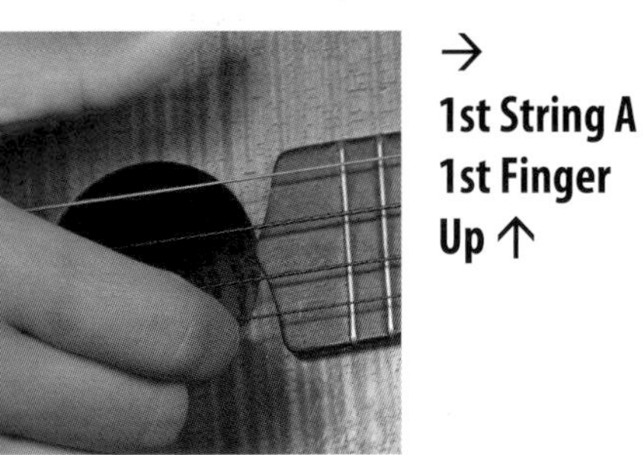

→
1st String A
1st Finger
Up ↑

Practice this sequence very slowly and carefully. Then, little by little, increase the speed until it begins to be a smooth phrase, **[down, down, up, down, up], [down, down, up, down, up],** and so on.

This will be a fine waltz (3/4) or 6/8 rhythm you can use to vary strumming.

Try your hand at picking with this well-known melody. The 3/4 rhythm is **down-down** -up, **down**-up-down, for each measure.

Greensleeves

Attributed to Henry VIII

Strumming Rhythms and Techniques—The Roll Strum

This is one of the most important strum techniques used in Hawaiian ‘ukulele playing. It is a colorful way of creating energy in the strum by rapidly striking the strings with the fingernails to create emphasis in the rhythm.

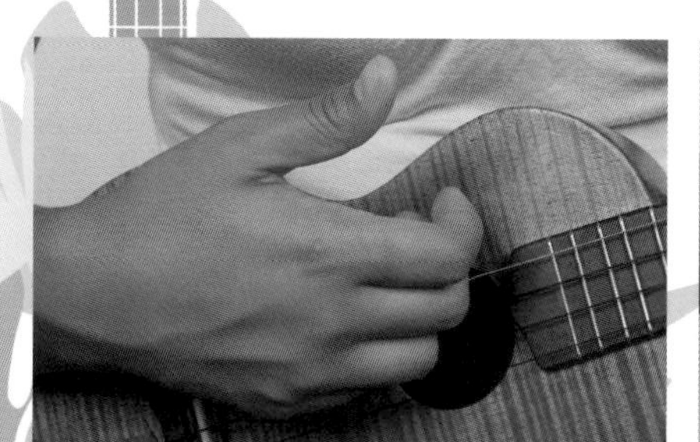

1. Start with the right hand relaxed and gently closed just above the 4th string.

2. Bring the hand down while opening the fingers. At the same time, strike the strings starting with the 4th fingernail, progressing to the last, the index finger.

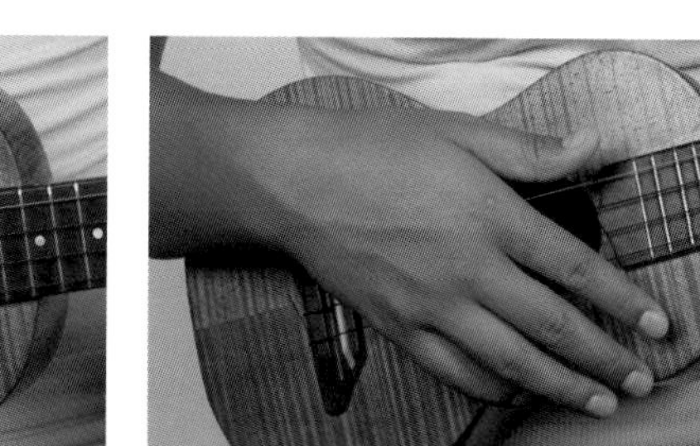

3. Make sure the hand uncurls like a fan and the fingernails strike the strings one after another!

It takes practice to strike the strings with separate fingers so you get a roll, not a single strum with four fingers at once.

The clue is that your hand should be open at the end. Imagine you are firmly flicking something off your leg! Another exercise is to open your left hand and try to roll strum the inside of your fingers as though they are the strings. Here, you can hold your hand up close to see how the right hand is “rolling” across the left hand fingers. Try this with a simple C chord first.

Roll Strum and A Minor Chords

Practice the roll strum with these chords once you are comfortable with the roll strum action and these chords.

Use the 8 x, 6 x, 4 x, 3 x, 2 x, and 1 x sequence to acquire finger memory and then try this rhythm: Roll strum on the **first beat** followed by 3 down strums (8 x and 4 x). Also roll strum on the **first beat** followed by two down strums for 6/4 and 3/4 time. When you are comfortable try one roll strum for each chord!

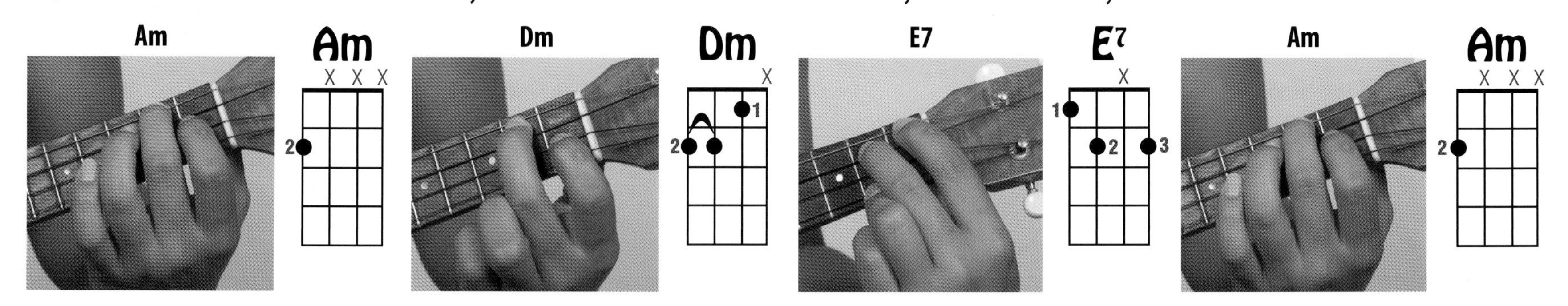

For the next piece, **"Drill Ye Tarriers,"** which has a strong first beat, practice using a roll strum at the beginning of each measure (see arrows on music). Then try the roll—at the beginning of each measure **followed by down↓ up ↑ strumming.**

Count and strum like this for each measure: ONE Roll down ↓, and ↑,Two ↓ , and ↑,Three ↓ , and ↑, Four ↓ , and ↑.

Then you can **bounce** the rhythm by making the downs longer and the ups shorter as in the rhythm of "**Hump**-ty, **Dum**[illegible]-ty."

Drill Ye Tarriers

Railroad Work Song

THE CALYPSO STRUM—This is a great strum pattern to spice up your rhythmic playing. It takes a little practice because you have to teach your right hand to do an "air" strum down (After DOWN, DOWN-UP (pause —air strum down) UP-DOWN-UP. Use the D major chord sequence.

DOWN | **DOWN – UP**   | Strum down ↓ **without** touching the strings | **UP** | **DOWN – UP**

Calypso Strum

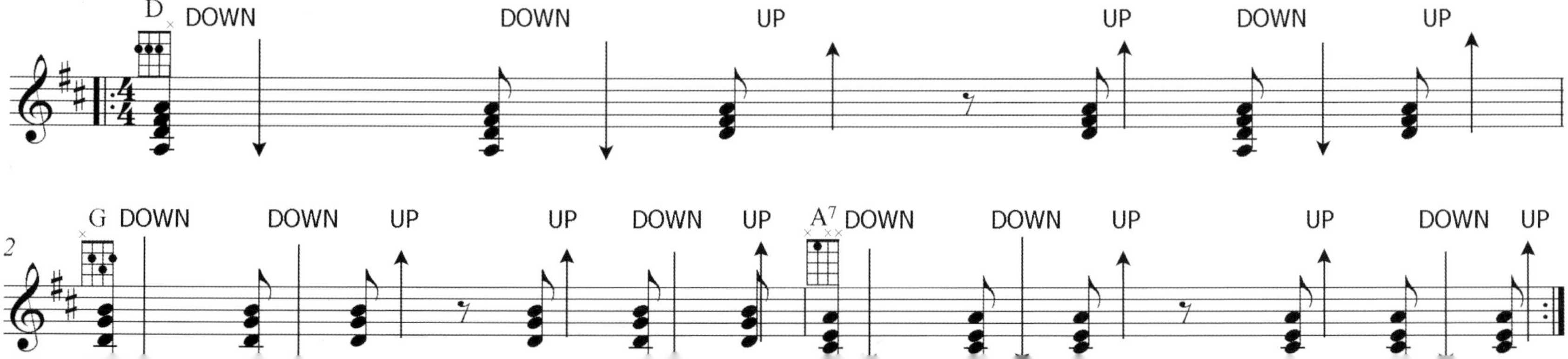

D DOWN DOWN UP UP DOWN UP

2 G DOWN DOWN UP UP DOWN UP A7 DOWN DOWN UP UP DOWN UP

Water Come A Me Eye

Jamaica Traditional

CRAZY G This famous jazz piece fits beautifully with the Calypso Rhythm except some measures have four, straight down-strums. These are easy to see because they have four quarter notes ♩♩♩♩ to each measure instead of a mix of quarter ♩ and eighth ♪ notes—♩ ♪ ♩ ♪ ♩. This great performance piece is a long one—part 1 is on these two pages and part 2 on the next two pages.

Crazy G

Traditional

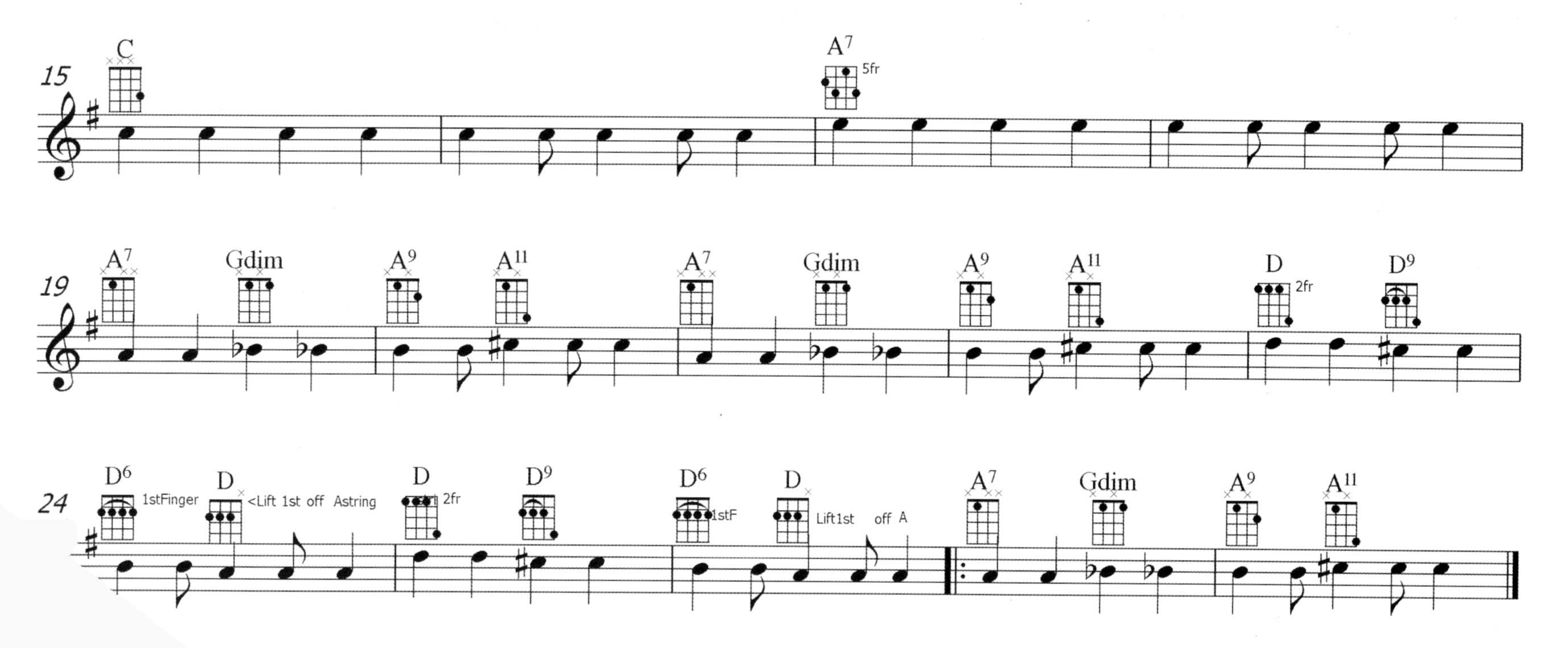
15
C
A7
5fr
19
A7
Gdim
A9
A11
A7
Gdim
A9
A11
D
2fr
D9
24
D6
1stFinger
D
<Lift 1st off Astring
D
2fr
D9
D6
1stF
D
Lift1st off A
A7
Gdim
A9
A11

Crazy G—Part Two

A NOTE ON playing A⁷ AND D CHORD SEQUENCE. These chords are not hard once you know how they progress! **In measures 9 and 10,** the D chord changes from **D,** to **D⁹** to **D⁶ simply by moving the notes on the A string** down the neck, one by one. Look at the chords of **A⁷** on measure 6. You hold the original **A⁷** on measure 5, add an extra note for **G dim** and then, one by one, using your third and 4th finger move down to **C♯dim** where your pinkie is on the 4th fret. Practice these changes first before you try to learn this 2nd half of "Crazy G."

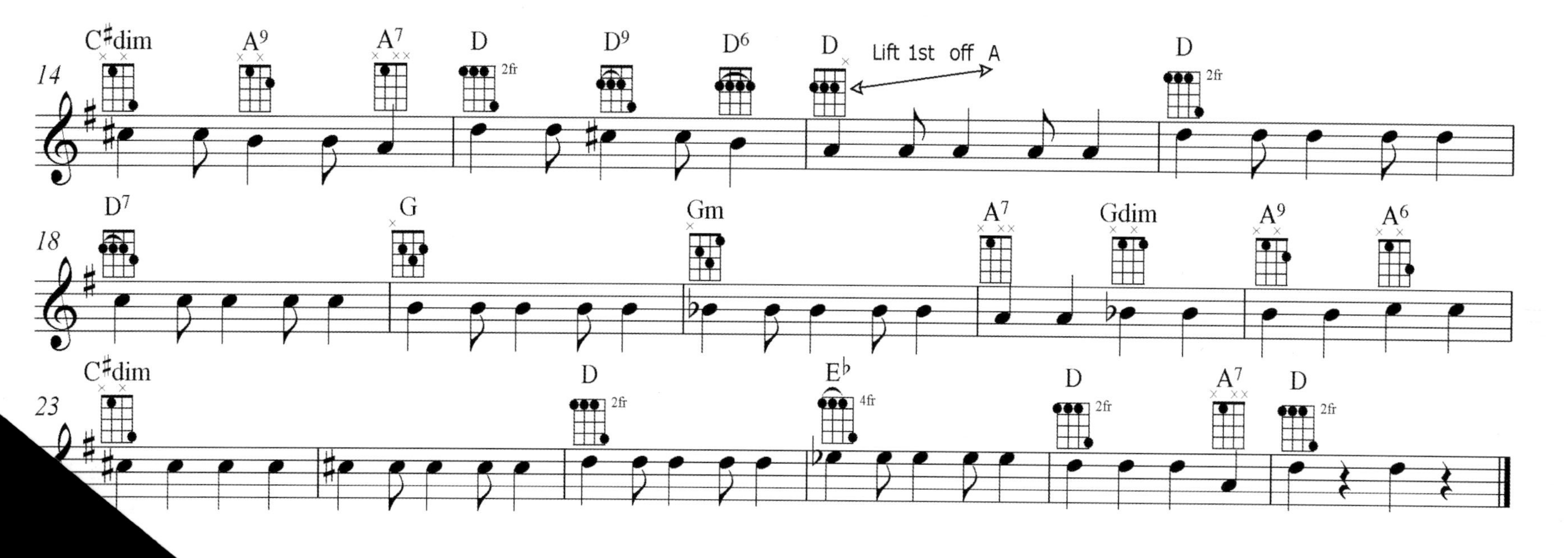
14
C♯dim
A9
A7
D
2fr
D9
D6
D
Lift 1st off A
D
2fr
18
D7
G
Gm
A7
Gdim
A9
A6
23
C♯dim
D
2fr
E♭
4fr
D
2fr
A7
D
2fr

The Triplet Strum

a lot more colorful if you are able to add triplet rhythms. The triplet is very common in folk music in many places, especially Irish dance music al.

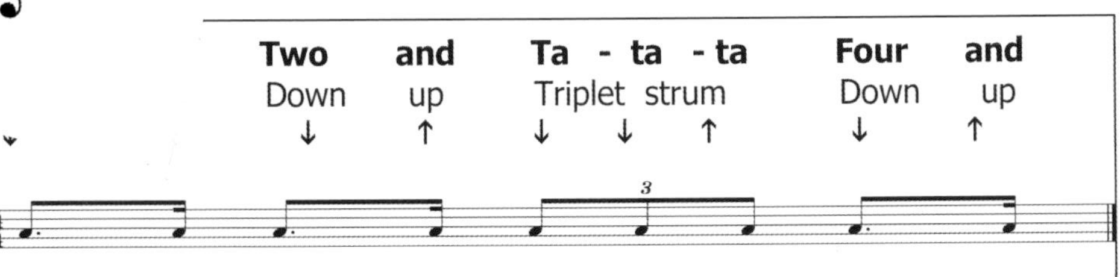

If we strum a 4/4 beat, the triplet can be put on any beat, but more usually on the **third beat.**

To achieve the triplet, which has to fit in three strums in one beat, do the following:

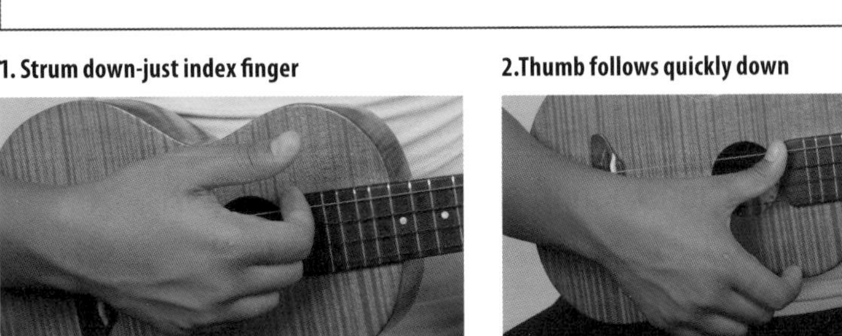

1. Strum down-just index finger

2.Thumb follows quickly down

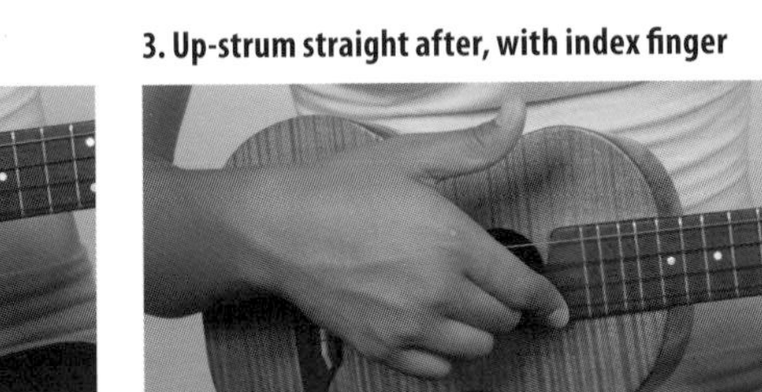

3. Up-strum straight after, with index finger

4. Continue down-up of index finger

Use a simple chord like the C chord to practice. Practice a little every day—it takes time for your finger memory to make it natural!

Using the Triplet Strum
First Down Beat Suggested
Polly Wolly Doodle
G
Triplet
Triplet
C
G
Oh, I went down South for to see my Sal, sing - ing Pol - ly Wo - ly Doo - dle all the
5
D7
Triplet
Triplet
day; My___ Sal she is a___ spunk - y gal, sing - ing Pol - ly Wol - ly Doo - dle all the
9
G
Triplet
C
G
D7
day. Fare thee well, fare thee well___ Fare thee well my fair - y fay, For I'm
14
Triplet
Triplet
D7
G
goin' to Loui - si - an - a, for to see my Su - sy - an - na, Sing - ing Pol - ly Wol - ly Doo - dle all the day.

Reggae Strumming

There are several Reggae strum patterns. Here are two that are easy to learn! Any Reggae strum relies on breaking up a strum rhythm by "damping" certain strums, in a regular strum sequence, to create a syncopated effect. In picture 3 below, you see the hand open, across the strings. When the hand makes contact with the strings it mutes them. This is called "damping."

1. DOWN ↓

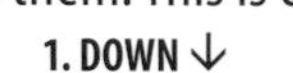

2. UP ↑

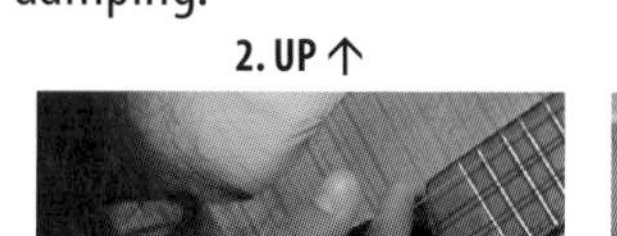

3. DAMP

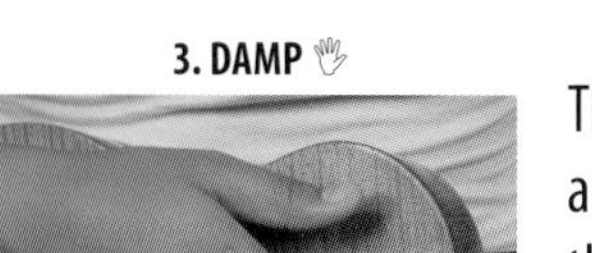

The first sequence is an **Down ↓ Up ↑ DAMP** . Strum down and back up, and then momentarily damp the strings, and immediately after the damp, start the same pattern again. The easiest way to damp at first is to open your hand and slap it down on the strings. This will make a contact sound against the wood, but that is ok at first. You will find the best position of your hand as you practice. In all practices, start very slow and gradually speed up as muscle memory takes over.

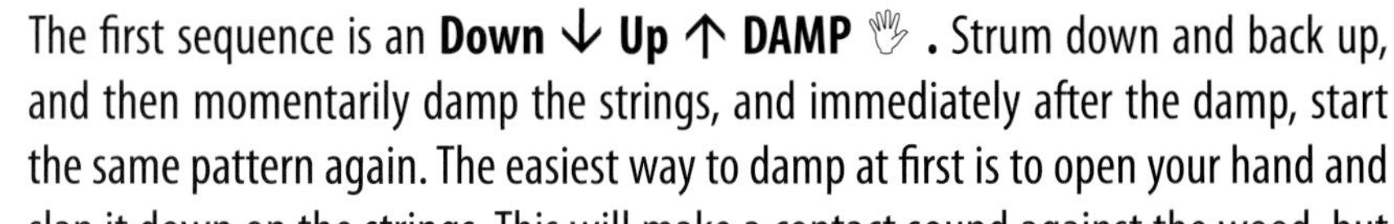

Second Reggae Strum: Up ↑ – Down ↓ – Up ↑ – Damp, Up ↑ – Down ↓ – Up ↑ – Damp and so on!

1. UP ↑ 2. DOWN ↓ 3. UP ↑ 4. DAMP

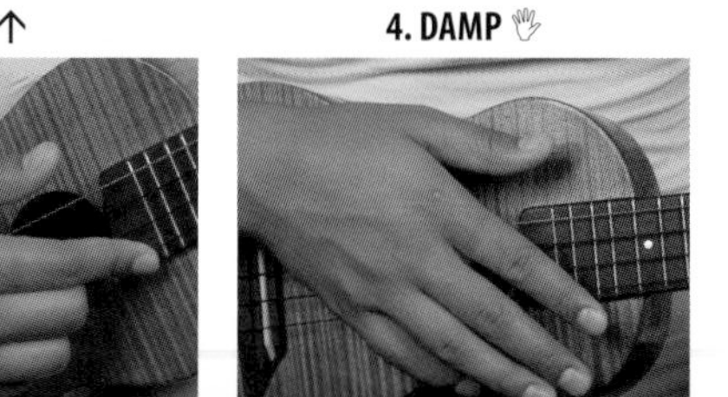

After practicing, try your hand at singing and strumming to **"Mango Walk"** on the next page, using the second strum pattern. You can find examples to listen to the song on YouTube. A steel band example would be good!

Reggae Strum
Mango Walk
Jamaican Calypso
C7 F C7 F
My bro-ther did a tell you not to go man - go wa - lk, go man - go wa - lk, go man - go walk My
5
C7 F C7
bro - ther did a tell you not to go man - go walk and don't steal the num - ber e -
9
C7 F C7 F
le - ven___ Tell me Joe, do tell me, do tell me, tell me, do tell me, tell me___
14
C7 F C7 F
Tell me Joe, do tell me, do tell me, Why did you steal num - ber 'le - ven?

The Thumb Roll Triplet Strum

The "thumb-roll" triplet uses the same pattern as the basic triplet strum, but the effect is different because the sound of the thumb rolling across the strings right behind the first finger creates a tighter, more blended triplet. The sequence below is the same, but the thumb **rolls down right behind the first finger,** in the down-strum of the triplet. **For the roll sound to work you must drag your thumb** across the strings so you hear them sounding almost one by one, but slightly quicker. Try the thumb action in slow motion at first, then slowly speed up!

The Thumb-Roll Triplet Strum—the sound is different as well as a slight rhythmic difference.

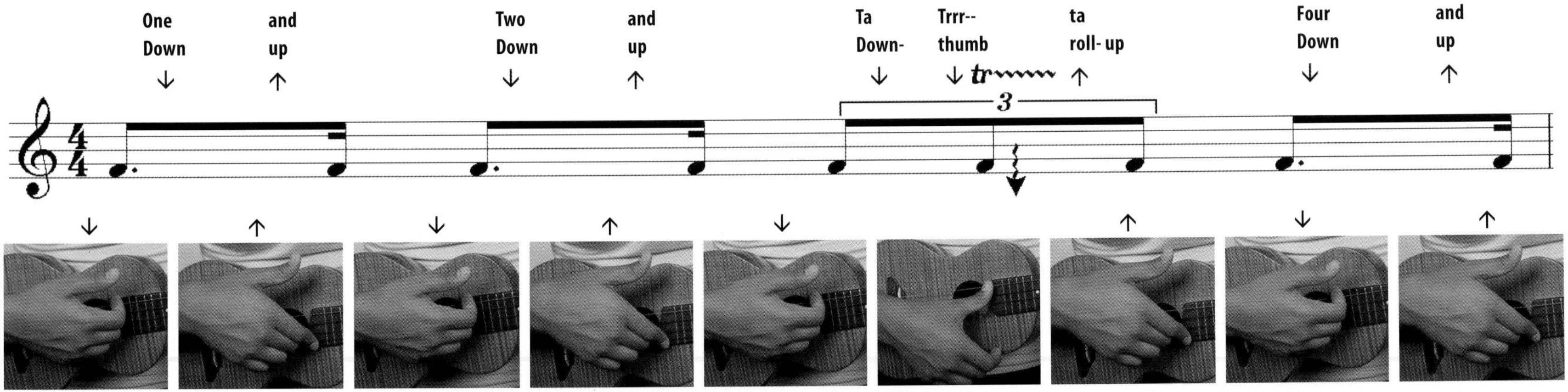

One Down ↓ | and up ↑ | Two Down ↓ | and up ↑ | Ta Down- ↓ | Trrr-- thumb ↓ trmmm | ta roll-up ↑ | Four Down ↓ | and up ↑

This pretty melody from Vanuatu has a rhythm that works well for the thumb roll triplet strum. Try the roll on longer notes like "bow" in measures 8/9 or for down-beats, like "children"–measure 10.

Live Aloha

Thumb-Finger Strumming—Using Thumb and First Finger

In the pictures below, **notice that your hand pivots on your 4th finger.** All the strums are achieved just using the thumb and first finger. In a regular, 4/4 rhythm, the 1st and 3rd beats are sounded by the thumb on the 4th string. Beats 2 and 4 are played up-down-up by the first finger on the other three strings. This sounds much better when you **bounce** the rhythm as in the words Hump-ty Dump-ty. Practice with open strings first (no chord).

One (thumb ↓ on 4th string)

And (Up ↑ with 1st finger)

Two (Down ↓ with 1st finger)

And (Up ↑ with 1st finger)

Three (Down ↓ with Thumb)

And (Up ↑ with 1st finger)

Four (Down ↓ with 1st finger)

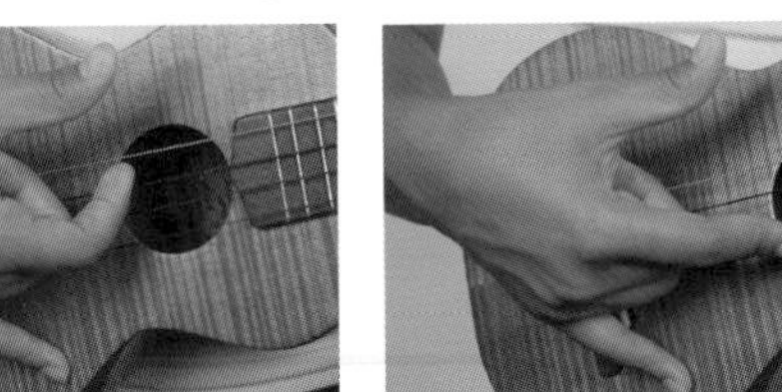

And (Up ↑ with 1st finger)

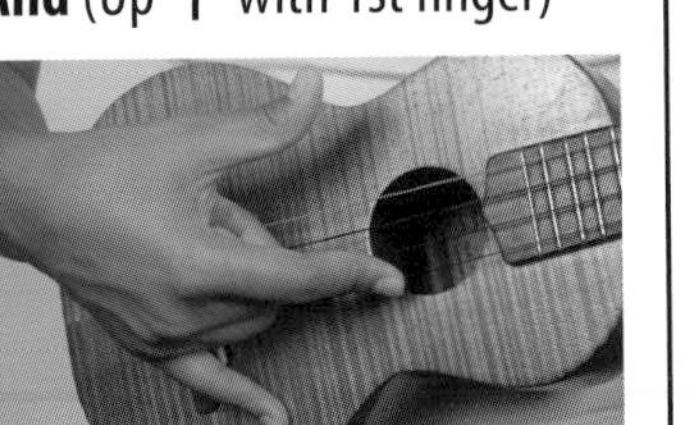

This rhythm becomes really interesting when you add a **triplet.** The triplet can come on the 2nd or 4th beat (when you are using your index finger). For the triplet on the 2nd beat for example: Go **Down** (thumb) then **up-down-up** with the index finger. You can vary this or triplet on both the 2nd and 4th beat.

Keys of B♭ and G Minor

B♭

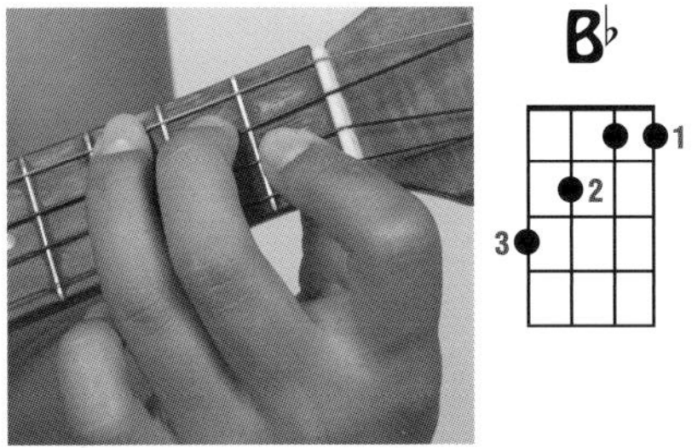

B♭

E♭

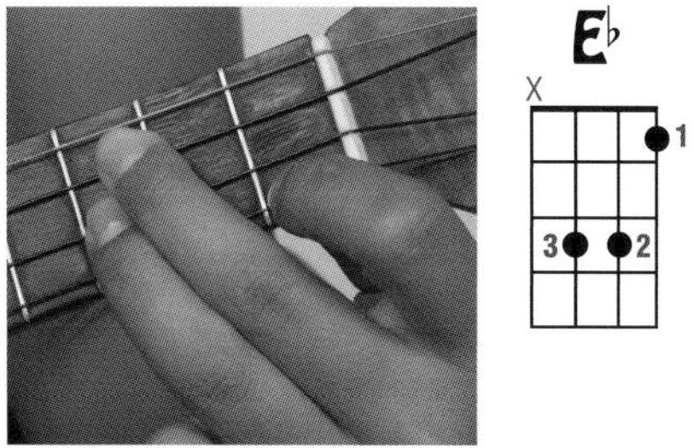

E♭

F^7

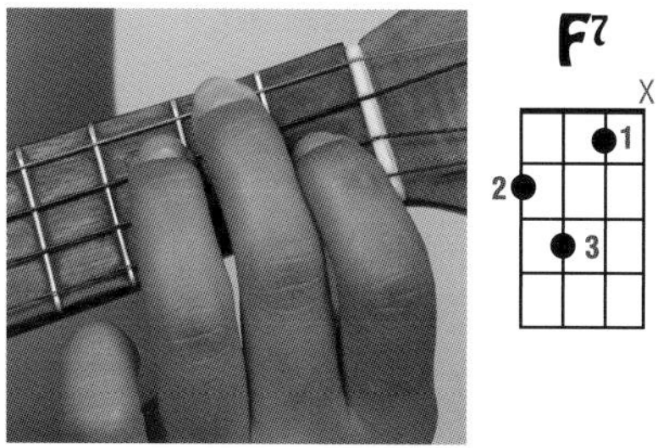

F^7

F^7 + 4th finger

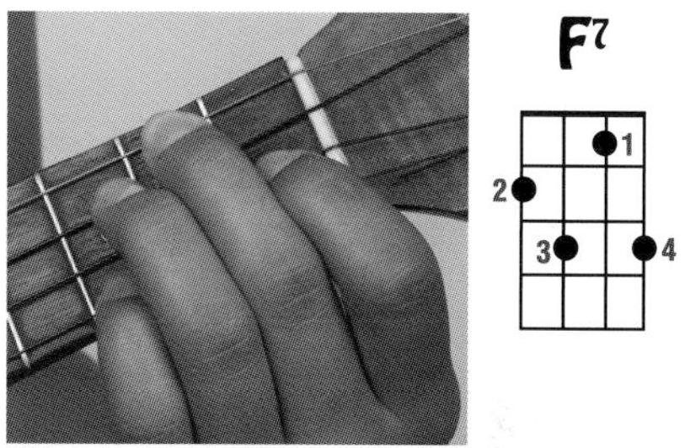

F^7

Gm

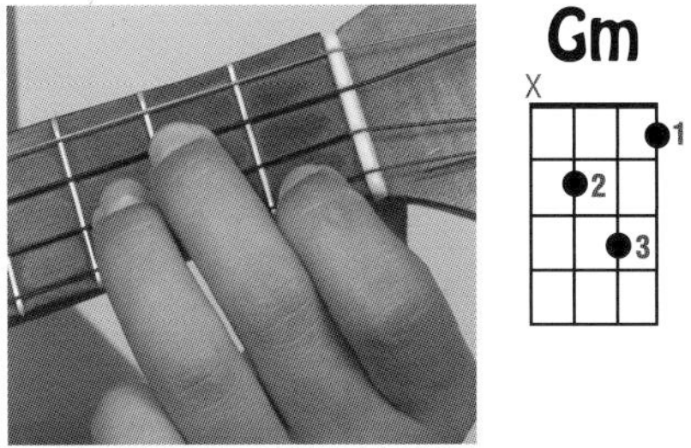

Gm

Cm

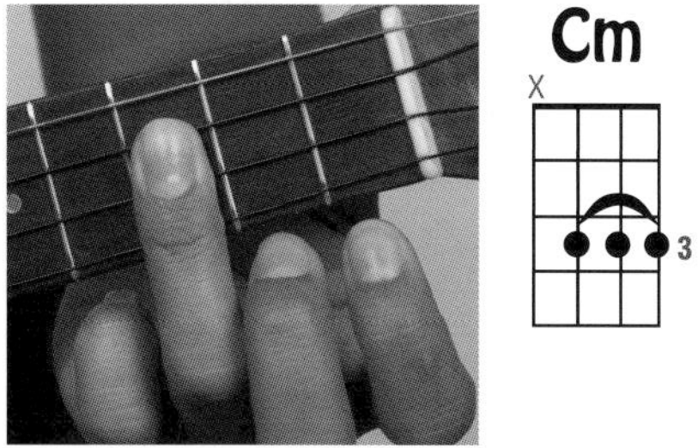

Cm

E♭^{7}

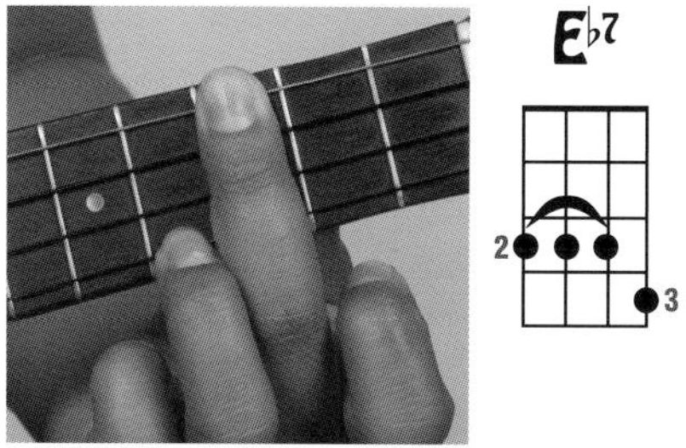

E♭^{7}

D^7

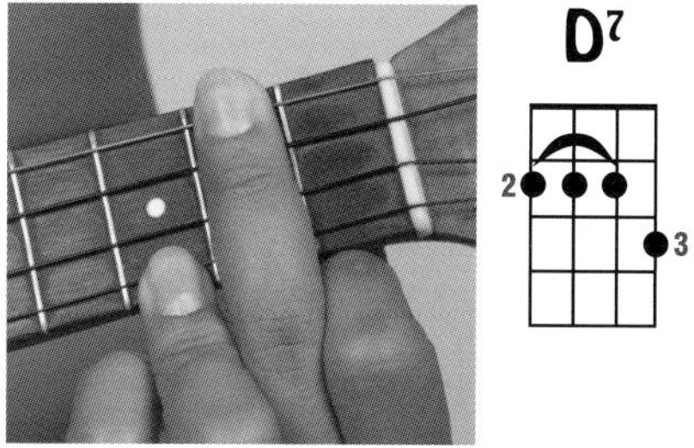

D^7

Practice these chords using the 8 x, 6 x, 4 x, 3 x, 2 x, 1 x method. Try any of the strum styles you have mastered to make the sequence more interesting! The next tune, an oldie when the 'ukulele was being popularized, has a great sequence of chords and a charming waltz lilt.

I'm Forever Blowing Bubbles
Jan Kenbrovin
I'm for-ev-er blow - ing bub- bles Pret - ty bub-bles in the air
They fly so high, near-ly reach the sky, then like my dreams they fade and die.
For - tune's al - ways hi - ding I've looked ev - 'ry where
I'm for-eve-er blow - ing bub- bles pre - tty bub - bles in the air

Tremolo

Most Hawaiian musicians who play melody, use tremolo, and nearly all Hawaiian professional musicians do this with the right thumb nail which has been allowed to grow, to act as a natural pick. However it **is** possible to play tremolo without having a long thumb nail! You need to buy a relatively soft or flexible pick, just a little stiffer than a yoghurt lid. In the islands of Vanuatu, I saw parrot-fish scales used as picks!

See the pictures below how to hold the pick. Your hand should be relaxed and the **thumb** holding the pick should be parallel to the strings. Again, make sure your pick is flexible.

1. Start with your right hand vertical, with your thumb nail facing you.

2. Place the pick ¾ way between the thumb and index finger.

3. Now, in regular strumming position, place the pick just above the string and lower it about 1/8 inch "into" the strings. Keep your thumb relaxed and parallel to the strings. Don't let your grip become claw-like and tense. Some players prefer to pivot the hand on the little finger.

Practice slowly at first on one note, (the A string is easiest) moving the pick up and down and gradually pick up speed. **It is very important to start off with a very flexible pick. For example, a nylon .46 mm pick works well.** A stiff pick will incorrectly make you feel you cannot do tremolo. If you don't have a pick on hand, cut a pick out from a yoghurt lid, though that is a tiny bit too flexible!

On the next page, try your hand at tremolo in this beautiful, Fijian farewell song! You can find many versions of this online.

Online are many versions of this
lovely farewell song from Fiji!
Isa Lei
Fijian Farewell
Tremolo=tr
C F C F C G C C F C Dm C G C G F C G C
I - sa I- sa vu- la- gi la - sa di- na No- mu la- ko au
(Ka - va) be- ka ko- a mai ca- ka- va No- mu la- ko au
7
na ra- ra wa - ki- na Ka - va I- sa le- i na - no ku ra- ra ra -
na se- ga - ni la- sa
14
wa- Ni - ki sa- na vo-du- e na ma- ta- ka, Bau na- nu- ma,
21
Play twice to finish
ralantando

Aloha 'Oe

Queen Liliuokalani
G C G D7 G C
Proud-ly glides the rain cloud o'er the cliffs, Blown on - ward by the gen tle breeze. How the scene re-calls the dis-tant
Ha - 'a heo ka ua i na pali, Ke ni - hi a 'ela i ka nahele, E hahai a - na pa - ha i - ka
7
G C D7 G G7 C G
past, And I live once a - gain my mem - o - ries. Fare - well to thee, fare - well to thee, O
liko, Pu - a 'a - hi - hi le - hua o u - ka. A - lo - ha 'oe, a - lo - ha 'oe, E
12
D7 G C G D7 G
beaut eous one who lives a - mong the flow - ers,
ke ona - on - a no - ho i ka li - po,
One fond em - brace be - fore I leave, un - til we meet a - gain.

Once you have learned these chords, you can easily find advanced chords online.

Common Chord Families

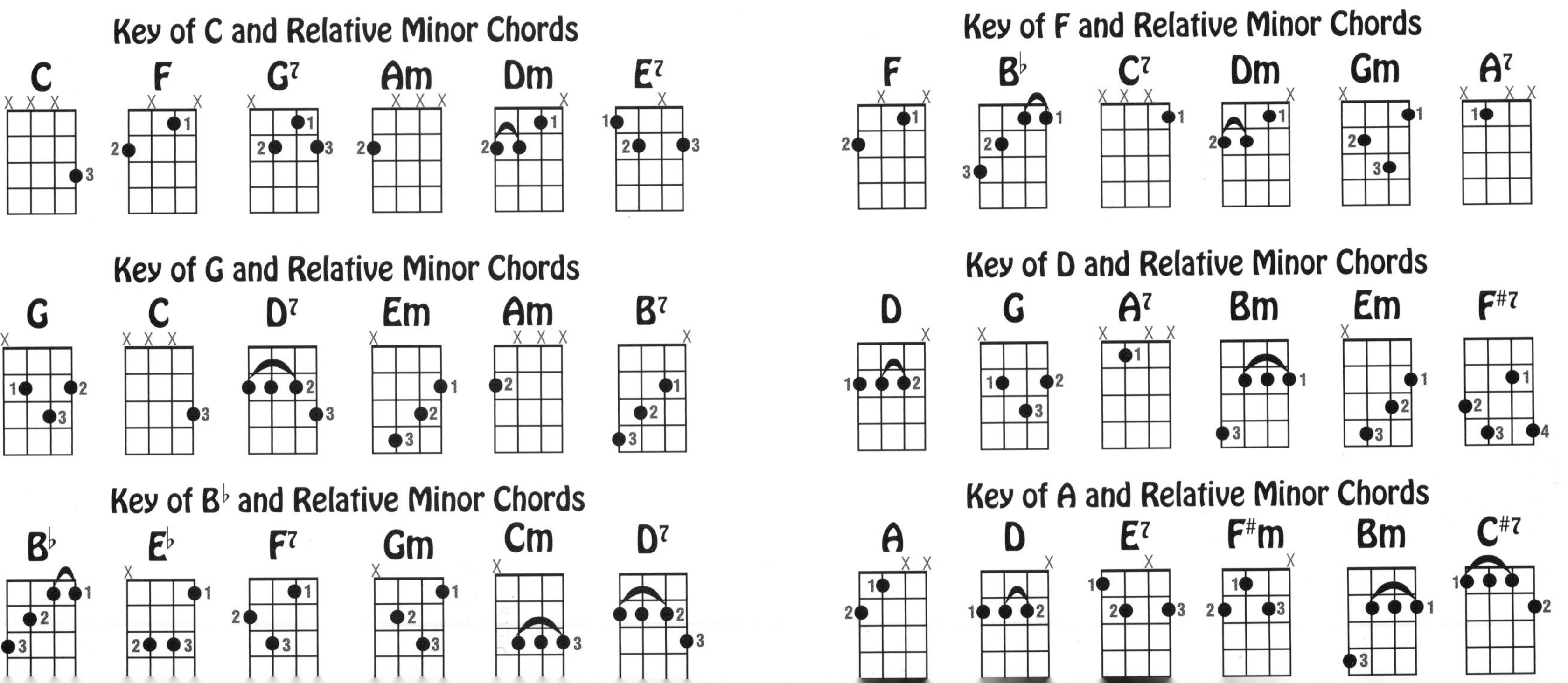